Fortitude
The Essential Guide To Building And Sustaining Mental Toughness

Kate Allgood

FORTITUDE: *The Essential Guide To Building And Sustaining Mental Toughness*

Copyright © 2017, 2021 Quantum Performance Inc

All rights reserved. No part of this book may be reproduced or transmitted in any form or by any means - graphic, electronic, or mechanical, including photocopying, recording, taping, or information storage and retrieval systems - without express written permission from the author. Please refer all pertinent questions to the author. Failure to comply with these terms may expose you to legal action and damages for copyright infringement.

The author of this book does not dispense medical advice or prescribe the use of any technique, either directly or indirectly, as a form of treatment for physical, emotional, or medical problems, without the advice of a physician. The author's intent is only to offer information of a general nature to help you in your quest for high performance. In the event you use any of the information in this book, the author and the publisher assume no responsibility for your actions.

Contact the Author
www.qpathlete.com

Praise For Fortitude

"Kate is a force in the sports business and with her new book she brings the best insight directly to your field of play."

~ **Jeremy M. Evans**
Founder of and Managing Attorney at California Sports Lawyer®

"As a business attorney, I have seen CEOs kill their businesses because they lacked the mental toughness to run their business with confidence. People want to do business with people who are confident. Kate's book is a must have for all who are in business as it is a guide for how to build mental toughness. A necessary skill required in business. Thank you for writing this book."

~ **Kelly Bagla**, Esq.
CEO of Bagla Law Firm, APC

"If you want to step up your game, your business or just kill it in life, "Fortitude: The essential Building Blocks of Mental Toughness" is an easy to read guide to do it. I've read and worked with Kate before, and she has helped me and my athletes understand how to be a better competitor, teammate and a leader. What I loved about this book was the simplicity to apply the concepts right away in my game, work and my life. As a youth coach this is priceless information that supports me to guide my athletes to reach peak performance, without being frustrated or overwhelmed."

~ **Majo Orellana**
Pro Athlete, Coach and Entrepreneur

"Through my work with thousands of athletes in rehabilitation and injury prevention training, I have discovered that physical skills alone will only take an athlete so far; he or she must also train the mind to excel at the top levels of sport. Kate Allgood is masterful in her ability to both toughen and refine the minds of athletes of all levels and enhance their performance on and off the field. I have high praise for Kate's strategies and *Fortitude: The Essential Building Blocks of Mental Toughness"*. This is a must-read for athletes and coaches seeking a competitive edge."

~ **Dave Gerbarg**, DPT CSCS TPI
President, Doctor of Physical Therapy
dave@oneninesportsmed.com

"Kate skillfully explains the value of mental toughness in the context of sports and athletics. As the founder and CEO of a high-performing and growing company, I see the potential to apply her thoughts in the business world."

~ **Helen Stevenson**
Founder and CEO, Reformulary Group Inc.

To my Dad, for everything you have done that has allowed my vision to become reality

Table Of Contents

Praise For Fortitude	iii
Table Of Contents	vii
Introduction	1
Who I Am	1
Why Should You Read This Book	3
Why I Chose To Write About Mental Toughness	5
Why You Should Understand The Building Blocks Of Mental Toughness	7
Chapter One: What Is Mental Toughness?	10
Defining Mental Toughness	10
What Are The Building Blocks Of Mental Toughness?	11
How You Can Apply What You Learn About Mental Toughness	13
Chapter Two: Confidence	15
Why Confidence Is Most Important	15
What Does Belief Have To Do With Confidence?	20
Can Trust Really Increase My Confidence?	25
Character - Integrity	26
How To Increase Integrity	29
Character - Intent	32

Competence Aspect Of Trust	34
Chapter Three: Motivation	**38**
What Is Motivation?	38
Building Motivation In Yourself And Others	41
Sustaining Motivation	44
Chapter Four: The Power Of Thinking Without Thinking	**48**
What Is Intuition?	48
What Does Intuition Have To Do With Mental Toughness?	50
How Can I Develop My Gut And Intuition?	52
Chapter Five: The Power Of Focus (Deep Practice)	**55**
All You Have Is This Moment	55
Myths About Focus	59
Meditation	62
Chapter Six: The Ability To Refocus	**66**
Flexibility Is Not Just For Your Body	66
The Challenges Of Refocusing	68
What Can I Do To Help Myself Refocus Better?	70
Chapter Seven: Mindfulness	**74**
What Is Mindfulness?	74
Why Do I Need To Figure Out My Own Mind?	75

How Is Mindfulness 77
   Related To Mental Toughness? 77
Conclusion 80
   How To Apply The Building Blocks Of Mental Toughness To Your Life 80
Notes 83

Introduction

"Mental toughness is more about what takes place off the field than on it."
~ John Wooden

Who I Am

Mental toughness isn't something I really started thinking about until after I stopped playing competitive ice hockey. For anyone who hasn't read my first book, I grew up an all-round athlete, playing any sport that was available to me and that I could put my hands on. The sport I took the furthest was ice hockey. I was fortunate to reach a very high participation level, playing in college and professionally as well as being pegged as a potential candidate for the 2010 Winter Olympics.

Along my path in hockey I won numerous awards and was recognized as one of the best female athletes across all sports at Canadian universities. The path wasn't without its obstacles; beginning at a very young age, I had several trying circumstances thrown my way that required a great deal of mental toughness. At the same time, as a friend once pointed out to me, these challenges used up my mental toughness. When it was all spent, I started to look at what mental toughness really was and how we can get it or regain it once it's been all used up.

As I researched this topic and the areas covered within this book, it become apparent very quickly why I had succeeded in something at a young age, and how those aspects continue to help me in life, albeit in a healthier way than they did before. When it came to hockey, my mental toughness was very solid and easy to tap into. I had confidence on the ice and a desire to have the puck on my stick when it mattered most. I had endless motivation; when I was young, my parents usually had to pull me off the ice. I was driven by the desire to get better, to see how good I could be.

As you will see later in the book, the ability to maintain a high level of focus came naturally to me. I didn't fall into peer pressure or anything else that would have distracted me from my goals. Out on the ice I allowed my instincts to come through. The interesting thing is that in other areas of my life, these characteristics were not present. When I analyze my career and life to see where I could have been better, I realize that one weakness was not having mental toughness in other aspects of my life.

As I mentioned previously, while growing up I had a lot going on in my personal life, and it eventually took its toll on hockey. This is why I know that, while it's great to have mental toughness in one area, if you don't have it throughout every

Fortitude

aspect of your life, eventually it will affect you. For some people, the characteristics of mental toughness come more easily, while others must work at it. No matter where you fall on the spectrum, it is important to understand the different aspects of mental toughness and where you need to work at it so that when a moment comes when you need it, the necessary mental fortitude will be at your disposal. You never know when that moment will come, so it's important to always be prepared and to know that you have what it takes to face the most difficult or trying circumstance in the best way possible, tapping into your inner strength.

Why Should You Read This Book

I wrote this book for a few reasons. First, as I have continuously worked with clients over the last few years, I have found that the topics I cover in this book are those that I am always discussing with them. As I began to dig deeper into the topics, I quickly found that these are the building blocks of mental toughness.

Mental toughness is a phrase that is thrown around a lot, especially in the world of athletics. It is a characteristic that people mention as being necessary for high performance. I couldn't agree more, but what is mental toughness really? This book sets out to answer this question and explain how we go about developing and nurturing our mental toughness.

The second reason I decided to write this book is that I felt it was time to build on my first book, *Get into the Zone: The Essential Guide to High Performance through Mental Training*. If you are new to the world of mental performance, I highly recommend that you read it before you jump into this book. My first book was designed to introduce and educate individuals about mental performance and mental training. It also presents elements of mental training that people can implement right away in a simple and concise manner. This book builds on those elements and takes a deeper look at the world of mental skills necessary for high performance. In essence, this book is more advanced than my first book in terms of the concepts and topics covered.

If you are looking to build mental toughness whether in sports, school, business or life, this book is for you. I have taken and researched concepts and topics from some of the best individuals in their fields, who look at what I consider to be the most essential building blocks for mental toughness. It is important to understand and implement the concepts in each part of your life to fully realize just how strong your mind can be.

As you will see, I have outlined six building blocks of mental toughness.

Fortitude

Why I Chose To Write About Mental Toughness

Although I touched upon this briefly in the previous sections, I will now go into the issue in more depth. I feel that people can benefit greatly by understanding the building blocks and what they can do to make them stronger. Life is not easy. Every day we need the ability to fight all the things in our world that are telling us we are not good enough, strong enough, brave enough, skilled enough, talented enough, pretty enough, etc. If we don't understand what skills we need to acquire to stay mentally strong, it is easy for everyday things, or stressors, to get the best of us. Then, when big things happen, it is nearly impossible to succeed because we have nothing left to pull from. This book is here to lift people to their full potential and to remind them that mental toughness is a skill – and that, like any skill, it must be understood, developed, and practiced. If you simply expect yourself to have what you need when you need it, you will likely face disappointment.

You never know when the moment will come when you need to be mentally tough; it will come at you out of the blue. In our affluent and relatively easy lives, mental toughness must be built and strengthened more than ever. One of the biggest reasons children struggle today is because of the often-held expectation that everything will be handed to them. From a very young age, many children are not taught how to overcome obstacles, and this hinders their ability to succeed in the world. Obstacles teach us about mental fortitude and help in the development of mental toughness. Without obstacles, society will develop a generation that doesn't have what it needs to thrive.

As I mentioned regarding myself, everyone could use more mental toughness. I have worked with some amazing athletes who are successful and confident, but they all still comment on the need for more confidence, motivation, and an ability to remain focused. The topics in this book are not just about mental toughness; they are the mental skills people need in their lives.

There are a number of things one can work on when it comes to the mind, but without addressing the topics covered in this book, it doesn't matter how much effort people put into those other areas—they won't experience their full impact. Visualization is an example of this point. Many people know the benefits of visualization and use it, sometimes even over-relying on it. Visualization is a great tool, and using it can definitely help with the topics in this book, but it isn't magic and can't do everything.

The clients I have worked with who are already confident, motivated, and focused achieve quicker and better results with visualization than do those who aren't. Visualization is great for maintaining the skills needed for mental toughness, but it helps a lot more if the skills already have a strong base and if visualization is used to support them as part of a whole package.

My hope in writing this book is to teach people about these characteristics in ways they haven't thought about before. The topics are not new; most people reading this know their importance, but learning about them in a different way can often lead to things clicking differently. There are no new concepts. Most people who do what I do know about these topics and teach them to their clients. We all have different ways of producing material and information, and I hope that the way I produce and display it will help people continue building awareness of these topics and increase their understanding.

Why You Should Understand The Building Blocks Of Mental Toughness

Like many things, knowledge is power. The more you know about something, the better position you are in to understand it and, from there, to do something with it. Increased understanding generally leads to increased awareness. While not specifically addressed in this book, awareness is key to developing and getting better at anything. Without awareness, change is very difficult.

You may have sufficient skills, talent, and knowledge, but if you don't know when and how to apply them to your situation, you will have a very low chance of succeeding at reaching your goals. This is one of the reasons why a big part of the work I do with clients involves helping them understand themselves. When people understand how they may react or perform in a certain situation, the better they become at preparing for it so that they can increase the probability it will go the way they hope and imagine—and, if necessary, change strategies before the event. Without such awareness, they go into the situation hoping for the best and feeling helpless, as though they have no power to change anything—when, in fact, they could if they had only been aware.

As mentioned earlier, in this day and age, I think that being aware of mental toughness is more important than ever. It's a skill that must be practiced and understood. Our minds set us apart from others; those who can harness the power of the mind, and do what others won't or can't do, are the ones who succeed in life. This book is just one in a list of valuable tools you can use in your quest to continue getting better.

Finally, I think people should understand the building blocks because the phrase "mental toughness" is thrown around so much; people should know what they are talking about. I hear about it all the time, the need to increase mental toughness, but when I ask people what that means, they have difficulty articulating it. This book will help clarify the concept and make it easier for you to communicate to others—such as your coach—what in particular you need help with in regards to mental toughness. Instead of saying, "I need to be more mentally tough," or, "My kid needs more mental toughness," you can say, "I need more confidence or motivation," or "I need to be able to refocus or my perfectionism will get in the way." This will make your goals clearer and more direct – and, consequently, you will have an easier time making the necessary changes.

Chapter One:
What Is Mental Toughness?

"Mental toughness is spartanism with qualities of sacrifice, self-denial, dedication. It is fearlessness, and it is love."
~ *Vince Lombardi*

Defining Mental Toughness

Mental toughness is a concept that is widely used, even overused, and it shouldn't be a surprise that its origins stem from sports. There are quite a few popular and effective definitions of mental toughness with the commonality among them stemming from the fact that mental toughness is looked upon as a combination of mental attributes. From reflecting on these definitions along with what I have discovered to date myself, I have defined mental toughness as:

"The natural or developed mental edge that results from a collection of skills, attributes, values, mindset, and behaviors that allow people to overcome any obstacle, adversity, or pressure as well as deal with the general day-to-day demands (lifestyle, training, competition) placed upon them and still remain consistent, focused, confident, and motivated to achieve their goals."

Fortitude

This book focuses on the skills, attributes, values, emotions, and behaviors of mental toughness and how one can develop this mental edge. There is no set way to look at mental toughness. The mental toughness people need for themselves in their situation is uniquely theirs, and this will make the definition slightly different from person to person. What is outlined above is not the one and only way to look at mental toughness but it is a guideline. I encourage you to use my definition as a framework from which you create your own definition based on what you think mental toughness is to you keeping in mind what you have experienced.

What Are The Building Blocks Of Mental Toughness?

The following chapters present the building blocks of mental toughness. They encompass the skills, attributes, values, mindset, and behaviors that must exist for people to have mental toughness and to use it to their advantage to achieve the goals and success they want. Each building block is usually interdependent on the rest. If you take away one, you can still have a lot going for you but your overall mental toughness will be affected.

Mental toughness can be measured, so if one area isn't developed it doesn't mean you don't have mental toughness; it just means you can develop it more. Remember, like any skill, mental toughness is something to develop over a period of time. Each period of your life might require a new level. You may have had the right level for your experiences in the past but now realize that it's time to develop more skill as your present situation requires it.

Think of the building blocks as being like a puzzle; each piece will fit differently for each person. It may even be that each piece is a different size for each person. There is no set rule or way in which the pieces must fit together; they just must fit together in some way. As you will see, confidence and refocusing are two of the most important components of mental toughness. They are number 1 and 2, respectively, in terms of important required mental skills. They are also usually the hardest ones to develop and sustain over an extended period of time.

As you read through each of the building blocks, make a quick analysis of your own level of this skill, attribute, mindset, value, or behavior and what you think you must improve in it. Also make sure you understand your situation clearly and what it demands of you. If you don't know your situation and what it demands of you, you won't know which building blocks are most important for you and, thus, which of them need more development. I have selected these building blocks based on my personal experience as well as what I have observed through my years of working with military personnel, business people, and clients at all levels of sports. To me, these building blocks are the fundamentals of mental toughness.

How You Can Apply What You Learn About Mental Toughness

As I mentioned previously, you should take this information as a guide. I believe these are the building blocks of mental toughness, but there might be one missing that you think you need. While acknowledging that every person is different, I know through the work I do with clients that these topics come up time and time again. They seem to be at the source of many of the issues I work with and are areas with which clients are looking for help.

I encourage each of you to apply each concept one by one. Really look to develop one of the following building blocks at a time. Once you feel as though you've gotten a handle on one of them, add and look to develop the next one. Trying to do them all at once will make the work unnecessarily hard; most likely you will become discouraged and stop putting in the work necessary to develop any of them. Working with these building blocks is a process; it can be a lifelong process. Each of these skills will continuously need to be developed over your lifetime.

There may be years between the times when you need to emphasize developing one of the areas, but eventually you will need to develop it more to become the person you need and want to be at that stage of your life. Each stage of your life presents different challenges. If you are not paying attention and continuously developing your mental toughness, you may not be the person you must be for the next challenge or situation in which you find yourself.

Chapter Two: Confidence

"Optimism is the faith that leads to achievement. Nothing can be done without hope and confidence."
~ Helen Keller

Why Confidence Is Most Important

Confidence is the most important component of mental toughness. It affects everything else, from motivation and decision-making to focus. Without confidence, the other factors are harder to develop and work on because they will always fall back on confidence. If you doubt yourself, it will be that much harder to motivate yourself to do the necessary work to reach the goal you have in mind. Doubt will pull your focus away from the task at hand and bring your focus internally to your negative mind and self-doubt. Success in sports relies on our ability to maintain focus on the cues around us, the things outside ourselves.

So, what exactly is confidence? One definition of self-confidence relates to self-assurance in one's personal judgment, ability, power, etc. To me, that is very broad and makes it difficult to really know how to increase self-confidence. Obviously, how things are going in our lives or the results of our performances can help us temporarily feel better about our abilities and judgments because we are getting a positive reinforcement that indicates they are strong. However, what happens when our environment is not going as we hoped or anticipated? What happens when we are in a slump? Well, self-confidence goes down as well because now doubt starts to creep in and we aren't sure about our abilities or judgment.

This is how most people experience self-confidence: a roller coaster ride that is usually highly dictated by what is happening in their lives. This puts self-confidence out of our control and makes it very difficult for us to do anything about it. One of the first questions I ask clients is, "How do you increase self-confidence?" Their response most of the time is, "Play better or get the results I want." That will definitely help boost confidence; however, often we need the confidence to play better and get the results we are looking for.

Given this situation, I view confidence as trust and belief in ourselves to such a high degree that no matter what occurs in our outer world, our confidence stays the course because our foundation is strong. What do I mean by foundation? Well, I have begun to look at confidence as a triangle, as seen in the diagram below. Confidence is at the top of the triangle. It is what we want to feel; however, trust and belief are at the bottom, forming the foundation for confidence. If we build trust and belief in ourselves. confidence will increase. The stronger the foundation, the more difficult it will be for something in our outside world to impact confidence in a negative way.

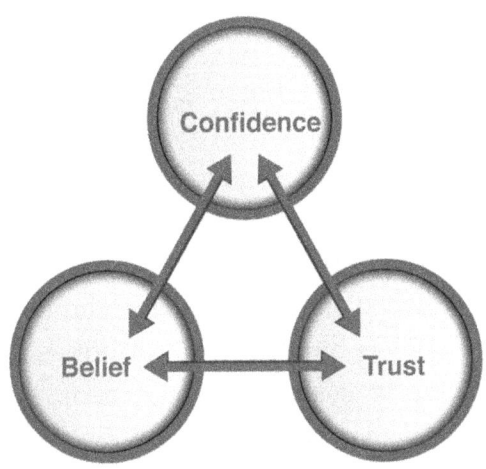

This foundation of belief and trust must be rock solid because every day we get messages that are telling us we are not good enough, strong enough, brave enough, smart enough, etc. These messages come from the media, social media, people in our lives, a failed test, missing the winning shot, etc. To counter the negative messages from the outside world we must create the strongest foundation we can. At first, for most people, this means building the foundation and then, over time, adding to it to maintain its strength.

In the next two sections I am going to look at belief and trust in depth but before I do, I want to point out that working on belief and trust takes a lot of effort, and is by no means something that will happen overnight. So, while you're working on these two foundational aspects of confidence, let's look at a few things you can do to build confidence and implement immediately.

The first is body posture. There is a wonderful TED Talk by Amy Cuddy, which I highly recommend watching, that goes in depth into body language and how it can shape who you are and change the way people view you. In the video, Amy talks about how our body language can change the level of two very important hormones when it comes to confidence. They are cortisol, our stress hormone, and testosterone, our dominance hormone. When we stand or sit in positions that open our bodies, such as what she calls the super hero pose (standing tall, feet apart, and hands on hips), our cortisol levels go down and our testosterone levels go up. This means that if you stand for approximately five minutes in a confident stance, you will start to feel more confident because your hormones change.

This is obviously the same for the opposite type of body language. If we cross our arms or legs, or stand or sit in postures that close off our bodies, our cortisol levels increase and our testosterone decreases. This means that we will start to feel more stressed. Think about how you naturally sit or stand when you are feeling confident, then take on that posture. How do you feel? Then do the same for when you are not feeling confident. Do you notice a difference? We go into these body poses without thinking about it. How we feel dictates how we stand or sit, and this occurs in the reverse scenario as described above. We can change how we feel by our body language. This is something that is very controllable and I encourage you to try it the next time you are feeling nervous or less than confident in anything. Spend some time standing with confidence.

Visualization is also a good tool to use. You can think of past positive performances to make you feel good about your abilities and skills and remind yourself that you are fully capable of tackling the task at hand. Watching videos, especially of yourself, is also an effective tool, once again to remind you of your skill set and that you have what you need to handle whatever is in front of you.

Positive affirmations are also helpful. It is important to speak to yourself in confident ways. Every time you do, you build pathways in your brain that make it easier to do so again in the future and to see things in ways that will continue boosting your confidence. Every situation has positive and negative aspects, but we must train our brain to pick out the good, the things we can build off to see what we are capable of.

Kate Allgood

What Does Belief Have To Do With Confidence?

Think about your belief systems for a moment. Do you know what they are? What immediately comes to mind? List some of them so you can see them and reflect on them. Our beliefs are at the core of our being. Often, we don't even know what they are, yet they play such a strong role in our actions and behavior. Sometimes this is because our beliefs are on a subconscious level, which can make it very difficult at times to know what beneath the surface is affecting what we see in our actions. Beliefs grow over time and create very strong roots, which can make them hard to change, but examining and possibly changing our beliefs is one of the first steps to building a strong foundation of confidence.

Actions and beliefs go hand in hand. If you are unsure what your beliefs are, look at your actions and behavior. Our actions confirm our beliefs. We act according to our beliefs and find evidence to support our beliefs. For example, I have a client who was injured a couple years ago and out of her sport for close to a year. Through this time and during the time when she was coming back and starting to play again, everyone around her kept giving her the message that it would take a long time to recover, that she might never be the player she once was and that she would be out of shape.

Fortitude

Recovering from an injury does take time, but through the messages she was receiving she started creating a belief about being out of shape. Even after she was fully recovered and had done a lot of work to become even stronger than she was before the injury, she had a belief that she was out of shape, and this belief was constantly reinforced because her actions and behavior suggested that she was out of shape when, in fact, she was perfectly in shape for her situation.

Could she continue to improve? Sure, but she had a lot more stamina and energy than she gave herself credit for. One of the reasons for this is that she found evidence to support the belief of her not being in shape. She could play a whole game feeling great and then in the last 15 minutes of the game start to lose her breath, and she took that one fact to support what she believed.

To better understand how beliefs affect our behaviors and actions, let's look at what a self-fulfilling prophecy is. Many people have heard this term and understand the general idea of what it means. Scientifically it is defined as the process by which one's expectations about a person eventually lead that person to behave in ways that confirm those expectations.

So, if you think about the fact that our perception of a person could lead to their behaving based on those expectations, imagine the expectations we have for ourselves and the impact they have on how we behave. Think about the expectations you have for yourself. If you expect bad results or a poor performance, you will behave in ways to confirm those beliefs. If you believe the opposite, you will start to act in ways that confirm you will have good results and perform well.

This is why beliefs are so important to confidence. Part of confidence is stitching together moments to see potential, to see what could be instead of what is broken. If you constantly behave and act in ways that support the things you don't want, you won't get many moments to stitch together to build the confidence you need to tackle the challenges ahead.

I challenge you to start investigating what your beliefs are and how they are either hindering you or helping you in terms of achieving what you want. To help you begin this investigation, I want to talk about two beliefs that absolutely must exist for true confidence to be built. Even if you changed all your other beliefs, these two are what matter the most and have the greatest impact on beliefs and confidence. Information about these beliefs and their impact comes from research done by Brené Brown; after reading this section, if you want to dive deeper, you should check out her book, *The Gifts of Imperfection*. The core beliefs you must have are:

Fortitude

1. The belief that it will all work out.
2. The belief that "I am enough."

Let's look at these two beliefs further, starting with the first belief, that it will all work out. If it hasn't, you haven't reached your destination. This is where faith comes in. No matter the context, research continuously shows that faith plays a large role in our confidence and ability to overcome obstacles in pursuit of our goals. There must be a strong underlying belief that things will work out in the end. This allows us to move through things when they don't go as we would like.

It requires understanding that often there is more at play than just ourselves and what we can control. It is trusting and understanding that sometimes the path or result we think is bad will turn out to be the best thing that ever happened. We cannot predict how one moment will affect our lives, so we must believe that, however something looks, we will get through it and the role that moment plays will be revealed when it is supposed to be.

According to Brown's research, faith is not necessarily about religion or spirituality. It is a place of mystery where we find the courage to believe in what we cannot see and the strength to let go of our fear of uncertainty. I like this definition because we all want certainty. One of the things I find most often when asking my clients about confidence is that they want certainty because that is what makes them feel confident. There is no certainty in life, so being able to get to a place where we believe that things will work out, and have faith in the unknown, letting go of the need for certainty and the fear that comes with it, gets us one step closer to the confidence we need in the pursuit of excellence.

Now let's look at the belief that "I am enough." This is very deep and complicated and not something into which I can delve fully in this book. However, this is a big one, especially for athletes and the identities they create around their sports and talent. "I am enough" is saying that, beyond results, scores, accolades, prizes, etc., you as a person are enough. Often, though, the opposite belief exists: "I am not enough." This leads athletes to chase after the next significant moment that will let them feel good enough, at least for a little while, until they focus on the next competition or game.

This belief creates a sports culture in which athletes feel they are only as good as their next performance. This is considered shame, and there is a lot of shame in the world of athletics, making it very difficult for an athlete to make a mistake. When an athlete does make a mistake, they see it outside the context of the situation; they become that mistake, they feel that the mistake reflects who they are. If we feel we are good enough, we can make mistakes and move on. We can see the mistakes for what they are, change what we must change, and move on. However, when we feel shame about a mistake, we can't move on. It builds and builds and our actions confirm our beliefs. Eventually, our self-worth is only as good as our performance.

So, start looking at your beliefs, especially your beliefs about the two things I just mentioned. This takes time, as I stated earlier, but clients I have worked with who truly know they are more than the things they do excel at performing better and have the confidence in themselves as people to reach their full potential. These people also have better balance in their lives and have an easier time moving on from their sport or career when it's over.

Can Trust Really Increase My Confidence?

The short answer is a big YES! This section will discuss exactly why that is and how to build trust within yourself to gain more confidence, as well as how you can help others instill more trust in you. According to Stephen Covey, author of *The Speed of Trust* (a book I highly recommend), trust is a combination of two elements; character and competence. If you are missing either element, you are lacking in trust. Each aspect has sub components that will be discussed throughout this chapter section. The first part we are going to look at is character, which is composed of integrity and intent. Then we will look at competence, which is composed of capabilities and results.

Character - Integrity

Integrity occurs when there is no gap between one's intent and behavior. This could be understood as living by one's values, not just professing them, which is what occurs a lot of the time. Usually people don't need to talk about their values if they exist. If someone must profess that they are loyal, there's a good chance they aren't. Their loyalty should come through in their actions and behaviors to the point that it doesn't need to be explicitly expressed.

Integrity is a core part of trust. If trust were a tree, integrity would be the roots. Integrity is often not visible but is vital to the health of the tree (trust), as well as to its strength and growth. Many of the things that give someone a high level of integrity are never seen or acknowledged. Integrity is a hard characteristic to explain but most of the time people have no problem identifying a person who has a high level of integrity as opposed to someone who does not.

So how does integrity come into play in sports? I love the example Stephen Covey gives of tennis player Andy Roddick. In 2005, Roddick was at the Italian Masters, and in his match against Fernando Verdasco from Spain he was in a situation in which Roddick had a match point in his favor. In Verdasco's second serve, the line judge called the ball "out", giving Roddick the win. Everyone was cheering and had concluded that Roddick had won the match.

However, Roddick didn't accept the point. He told the judge the ball had been in and showed the judge the slight indentation on the clay court, which showed the ball had landed on the line—which in tennis means it's counted as in. The umpire allowed Roddick to overrule him and the point was given to Verdasco. Verdasco ended up winning the match. Andy Roddick lost the match that day but he gained trust and showed the utmost integrity in that situation. This, of course, would help him throughout his career because whenever he challenged a call in the future, the umpires would give much more credibility and respect to the challenge, which could work in Roddick's favor.

On the opposite end of the scale, when athletes lack integrity, they usually believe the ends justify the means. Doping is a perfect example of this. It is also a great example of how you need both character and competence to have trust. When athletes dope, they forget about the character part and focus only on the competent part, on increasing their capabilities and getting the results they want.

However, they lack integrity in the process. Think of the athletes who have been caught doping. They may have won many medals, awards, and competitions. They may have been labeled as some of the best athletes of all time or for a generation ... and then as soon as it was discovered they had been doping, everything—and I mean everything—was taken away. The respect they had, awards, financial aspects ... many things in their lives change. In some cases, they must pay back people who gave them money based on their reputations and results, and they are never regarded the same way again.

So how is integrity lost or maybe not as solid as it should be? Some of the biggest factors affecting integrity are boundaries. Brené Brown has a wonderful video she posted on YouTube that talks about how without proper boundaries we lose our integrity. What does this mean? Well, boundaries are our ability to know our limits, to know what types of behaviors we will accept in ourselves and from others, holding ourselves and other people accountable to the accepted behaviors.

Boundaries are not easy to hold, especially if as children we were never taught proper ones. However, they are imperative to our happiness and to holding on to our integrity. If you are a people pleaser, this is especially true. If you are saying yes to something and you really don't want to be doing it, you aren't holding on to proper boundaries;

Fortitude

eventually you become resentful and start to act in ways that don't match your integrity. Sometimes you must be less "nice" in the moment to be kinder in the long term and hold on to your integrity.

Another aspect of integrity is humility. The top leaders in the world know that there is a paradoxical blend between personal humility and professional will. Those with high integrity don't have a win-lose mentality or arrogance; they have and act upon principles above self, making sure they preserve the right blend to succeed and doing so with high levels of integrity.

Now that you know a bit more about integrity and its role in trust and confidence, you might be asking yourself how you can go about increasing your integrity. I'm glad you did because now I will go into some of the methods to do just that.

How To Increase Integrity

1. Reliability

When talking about reliability, I am not speaking of your reliability with others or how they perceive your reliability; I am talking about your own reliability to yourself.

In other words, when you make a commitment to yourself, keep it. Too often we make commitments to ourselves and don't follow through.

Each time we do this, we are decreasing our own reliability, and thus our integrity. This, in turn, hurts our trust of ourselves and ultimately our confidence. Breaking small commitments will make you second guess whether you can keep big commitments. How you do the small things in life will reflect on the larger things. Think about your reliability and how well you keep commitments to yourself. This is one of the areas you can start working on if you are looking to build integrity.

2. Identify Your Values

I make a point of addressing someone's values when they work with me. Often, people aren't sure what their values are or know what they are, but have fallen off track with them.

For someone to have good integrity, they must have values and know what they are. It is important to know what you stand for and to stand for it so that others know. As Mahatma Gandhi said, "To believe in something, and not to live it, is dishonest."

So, figure out what you stand for. This can take the form of listing your values (as I suggested above with beliefs) and stating what they mean and why they are your values, or even creating a mission statement, which can be for any area of your life—a written expression of what you stand for and how you want to live your life.

3. Be Open

Being open to new ideas, opinions, or points of view is important for integrity. Being closed-minded will not help you increase your integrity. As mentioned earlier, part of having a high level of integrity is humility—eliminating arrogance and the need to be right or to win. We must be humble enough to know that we do not have all the answers and that even if we have a strong opinion, we should be open to learning something new about the topic that might change our opinion. We can still stand for something and be open to the possibility that we don't know everything. If there is a specific area of your life where you feel you are more closed-minded, try to open your mind and see how there is more to know than you currently do. Believe me, the more open you are to new ideas and possibilities, the more trust will be extended to you than if you are closed-minded.

Character - Intent

Intent is the motive, agenda, and behavior behind an action. As I mentioned in the section on integrity, one's intent is also important for one's integrity. We want to come from a place where our motives, agendas, and behaviors are in alignment with one another. At the core of good intent are two things: caring and doing things that are mutually beneficial. When people come from a place of caring, and not selfishness, their intent is usually in the right place. As humans, we generally want people to judge us based on our intent but we judge others on their behavior. How we build good intent comes from three things.

1. **Examine and refine:** We must constantly examine our intent and refine what must be changed if it no longer serves what we want. It is easy for our intent to get altered in ways we don't want. I myself have thought that I had a good intention towards something, but upon further examination I realized my intent didn't match how I wanted to be or act. Sometimes things happen that make us jaded or hurt, and this changes the core motive behind our actions. So, we must constantly look and make sure we are coming from a place of caring in the best interest of ourselves and others.

Fortitude

2. **Non-judgment**: Sometimes things are what they seem but often they are not. This goes for both others' actions and our own. We often react so quickly based on the actions of someone or ourselves that we don't take the time to see the intent behind the behavior. We judge our behavior very quickly, often not taking the time to see the intent or motive behind it. If we actually took the time to understand what was behind the behavior, we would probably judge ourselves less harshly. Non-judgment is about finding a way to not judge ourselves for the things we do and to instead look further and see what is behind the action. Often the good intent or motive is there but it just isn't coming through, and that's okay. We may just need to find a way for our behavior to match the intent.

3. **Generosity:** It is important to think generous thoughts about ourselves. This goes hand in hand with non-judgment. If we are generous in our thinking towards ourselves, and don't just think the worst of ourselves right away, many misunderstandings can be resolved. It is then easier to make the corrections that must be made.

Competence Aspect Of Trust

I started with the character aspects of trust, which accompany us wherever we are. Competence, however, will change from circumstance to circumstance. The following part looks at what the competence aspect of trust encompasses and how to increase it.

The first part of competence is capabilities. We must feel we have the right capabilities to feel confident in a situation. How we do that is based on our talents, skills, attitudes, and knowledge. The more these four things line up with what we are doing, the more confidence we will feel and the better we will tend to perform. Let's look at each of these components.

Talents: This is different from skills because talent is generally viewed as natural, something we are better at than most people and have always had. It doesn't mean we don't need to work hard to develop it, and it is definitely something to develop. It is beneficial to develop our talents because they are our strengths; the more we rely on our strengths, the better we are at handling a situation and the more we set ourselves apart from others. We all have limitations or weaknesses we must work on, but we can't forget about the strengths because we develop these; we can make great strides and succeed where others don't.

Skills: These are also strengths but unlike talents they are specific things we have had to develop and work on. For instance, skating in hockey is a skill of mine. I worked extremely hard at it and now it's a strength, but I wasn't a natural skater originally. I developed my ability to skate as well as my talents of stick handling and my hockey IQ so I could set myself apart while I worked on my limitations. It is important to know the skills we need in a situation and how to develop them. The more our skills are in line with what is required, the easier it is to perform.

Knowledge: This is the information we need at our disposal to perform to our potential within a situation. The more knowledge we have, the better we will be. A lack of knowledge will lead to our not knowing what specific things we require to be successful. When we develop our knowledge base, we have more at our disposal and a better chance of making sound decisions.

Attitude: This is not about having a good or bad attitude; it is about the mindset we need for a specific situation. For example, each sport needs a different mindset. Some sports need a calmer, more relaxed,

Zen-like mindset, while others need more aggression, high tempo, and energy. Different situations require different attitudes and it is important to know if the attitude you have matches what it must be for a situation.

The more these four things match a given situation, the more capable we will feel. If you are lacking trust in yourself for the capabilities you need for something, you must go through these four things. List your talents, skills, knowledge, and attitude and determine whether they are a good fit for what you are doing. If they are not, figure out what you must change or add so they're where they need to be and so you feel more competent in what you are doing.

Another aspect of the competency part of trust is results. Results are not everything but they are important. At the end of the day you can have great character and the capabilities you need; however, if you aren't getting the results, something needs to change and you will lack trust in yourself for not coming through. Sometimes what must change is your approach—to become creative and find new ways of getting what you want. Don't cheat or do something illegal or unethical, but ultimately find a way to get results. Those who do so are rewarded. It doesn't always have to look pretty

Fortitude

or be the way you thought it should be or follow the path you thought it should take; just get the results.

If you find yourself lacking confidence, I hope this chapter has provided you with some useful starting points for deciding what you can do to build the confidence you want and need. It takes time, so be patient and know that each choice and situation provides an opportunity to build or break your own confidence, which might ultimately impact you in a crucial moment, when you need it most.

Chapter Three: Motivation

"Continuous effort - not strength or intelligence - is the key to unlocking our potential."
~ Liane Cardes

What Is Motivation?

I find motivation to be a word, much like integrity, that people know about without really understanding its definition. If you don't know exactly what it means, and the role it plays, it becomes very difficult to use—and, more importantly, to build and sustain. Motivation is very important for mental toughness because it is the ignition for all the energy a person needs to do anything. Being successful or achieving a big goal requires an enormous amount of time and energy. It is impossible to maintain the energy we need without the proper implementation of motivation.

Motivation is about understanding the internal and external motivators that must exist to keep ourselves focused, working hard, and maintaining the commitment we need to get where we want to go. Motivating ourselves and doing something because of our own internal drivers is important. It is necessary to be motivated for the simple pleasures and joys life offers or to simply develop and learn.

These are great motivators, and much of the time I must work on them with clients because they have become more focused on external motivators, such as winning, external approval, scholarships, and awards.

There is nothing wrong with external motivators but they won't provide the energy necessary to sustain the work and will also usually lead to a loss of fun and joy. The same is true for internal motivators; it is extremely hard to keep motivation going just because something is fun. The amount of effort required to reach a high level of performance will make the journey tedious at times, so if fun is your only motivator, you may encounter problems moving through the difficult moments.

So, what is motivation? As I mentioned previously, it is the source of ignition to supply the energy we need. More specifically, it works through flashes of images and emotions that allow us to tap into evolutionary neural programs connected to the mind's vast reserves of energy and attention. This means the proper form of motivation connects to a level of energy and attention that far surpasses what we have at our disposal on a day-to-day basis and allows us to sustain everything we must do over an extended period of time. Let's look at a couple of examples for help in understanding this.

Much of the time, motivation that seems internal in nature actually stems from an external source that simply taps into this evolutionary reserve of energy and attention, which then ignites the motivation for a person. Being the hockey player and fan that I am, the first example I want to provide is that of hockey goalies coming from Quebec, a province in Canada.

Back in the 1980s, a goalie from Quebec named Patrick Roy became the best goalie in the NHL. Roy served as a role model for young hockey players from Quebec and ignited within them a passion for being a goalie rather than playing another position. It took a few years but there was a massive influx of talented Quebec goalies because of this. This influx didn't sustain itself over a long period of time but it did for a specific generation that looked up to Roy. This is true for many other sports figures who have had major success. What we start seeing a few years later is a massive influx of players from that area.

This occurs because it creates motivation and passion in a person on a very deep level and can ignite in them the notion of "If *they* can do it, so can I." This is very powerful and leads to my second example. Before Roger Bannister broke the four-minute mile, people thought it was impossible, but as soon as he broke it, there was a flood of others who did so as well. He represented a source of motivation that ignited others and sparked them to do the same thing he did. His feat created a message for others: "You can do this too."

When we see others to whom we relate accomplishing things, we see that it's possible; this can provide the motivation necessary to ignite the energy we require to accomplish it too. The external trigger creates a strong internal spark that ignites the necessary motivation.

Building Motivation In Yourself And Others

Motivation, whether within yourself or within others, comes from a way of thinking, from specific types of words, and from tapping into what's known as primal cue psychology, a deep form of motivation that can help ignite and sustain what is needed.

Let's start with a certain mindset. Research by Daniel Coyle, author of *The Talent Code*, shows that a simple question can predict progress resulting from the amount of motivation a person has for the work they are doing. This question is, "How long do you think you will play?" The answer to this simple question provides an understanding of the commitment level of the person. Depending on the answer, it indicates either high or low commitment levels. Those with a high level of commitment generally outperform those with a low level of commitment even when the lesser committed person practices significantly more.

This illustrates the importance of the self-perspective the individual has from the beginning and shows that the mentality one maintains at the outset is far more important than the amount of practice and coaching. Another reason for the importance of the right mindset when it comes to motivation will be explored further in the chapter on focus, but know that more committed individuals have an easier time getting to a depth of practice and focus necessary to excel than do lower commitment individuals.

Let's now look at building motivation through specific language and words. This will particularly help those who are in a position of trying to motivate others. Dr. Carol Dweck has researched the language people use as it relates to motivation and performance and has revealed the importance of language that affirms effort and slow progress rather than innate talent or intelligence.

In her research, she looked at children and test taking. She took a sample of children and had them take a test that consisted of easy puzzles. After the initial test, the researchers gave the students their scores and added a single six-word sentence of praise. Half the children were praised for their effort ("You must have worked really hard") and the other half for their intelligence ("You must be smart at this"). The children were then tested a second time and were offered a choice between taking an easier or a harder test.

Of the children who were praised for their effort, 90 percent chose the harder test. Most of the children who were praised for their intelligence chose the easier test. The reason for this, Dweck states in her research, is that when we praise children for their intelligence, we are sending them the message that the "name of the game is look smart, don't risk making mistakes."

A third test was then given, which was uniformly harder. None of the kids did very well; however, how the kids were praised after the initial test affected how they responded to the situation. The group that had been praised for effort worked hard, dug in, looked for solutions, tested strategies, and overall was more involved in the test—and mentioned enjoying the test. The group that had been praised for its intelligence did not like the test, and viewed it as an indication that they weren't smart.

A fourth round of testing took place, with this test returning to the same difficulty as the initial test. The students who had been praised for their intelligence scored 20 percent lower than they did on their initial test, while the praised-for-effort group improved their scores by 30 percent from the initial test.

All this shows the importance of using language that supports effort and not talent or intelligence. When we try to motivate through language, we must go deeper than just "You are the best." We must tap into effort: "You worked hard," or "Good job." All the experts acknowledge that praise should not be given constantly but only when earned, as praise all the time can actually decrease motivation. This is something that has become a challenge in this day and age, when there are participation trophies and children are learning they don't have to earn a reward. This practice actually decreases their motivation to do what is necessary to succeed. The message they are receiving isn't about the importance of effort or progress and it's robbing them of the motivation they need.

Sustaining Motivation

Sustaining motivation can be very difficult at times. This is why it is so important to have the right motivation or combination of motivations. If you are motivated only by the fun or joy of something, it is often hard to keep that going through the difficult, less-than-fun moments. When you are seeking to excel, be great, and get to a long-term goal, the journey is not always fun or enjoyable; thus, there must be something to push you through those moments so you can keep moving forward.

Fortitude

Now, on the other hand, if you are not motivated by fun or enjoyment, it becomes hard to sustain the motivation because you grow tired and drained. For example, if you are doing something only for the money, it is very difficult to keep doing things for the result of getting a certain amount of cash. You must enjoy the process to really keep moving forward.

One of the things I find that often causes an inability to sustain motivation is a lack of fun. I often have conversations with clients about why they first started doing something and whether that reason was still something they thought about or were aware of. One of the things I learned late in my career—and that I wish I had kept more at the forefront of my mind throughout my career—was the reason why I decided to play hockey in the first place and why I chose that sport out of the many I could have focused on to be the sport I put the most time, energy, and effort into.

I came across a quote about playing for the girl who picked up the stick and fell in love with the game. That struck a chord with me at a time when I needed it the most, and it shifted my perspective. While things did not get easier, the quote eased my mind and showed me how I was looking at things. It is something that, had I thought about it long before I did, could have helped me keep my motivation going and enjoy the process more.

Other things that are important for sustaining motivation are rest, space, and time. Often people expend everything they have and don't find ways to refill, so they eventually get to a point where they have nothing left to give. For most high performers, this is hard and it's something I definitely struggled with at times—and something I sometimes struggle with to this day. You feel like you can't let up, you can't take your foot off the gas pedal, that resting means someone else will surpass you. However, I have learned that while hard work is necessary, so is rest.

Rest often allows us to go harder and better when we are doing what needs to be done than if we try to sustain our effort long after we have an empty gas tank. In any area of my life, I generally now know when I need a break to refuel. If I don't, my productivity and level of work performance go way down. If, however, I give myself a break, I come back feeling hungrier and more motivated than ever to keep pushing forward. So, make sure you know where your limits are and what you need so you can keep going over the long haul. Success is a marathon, and we must learn how long we can sprint within the marathon before taking a break to then sprint again.

The final thing I want to say about sustaining motivation is that, beyond taking breaks and doing something for the fun of it, you need some form of external motivating factor as well. Something that helps push you or inspire you. Competition is not a bad thing if it's healthy; surrounding yourself with others who push you or make you want to be better is good.

I remember playing in college and knowing there was a teammate right behind me, waiting to take my spot if I slowed down. It kept me on my toes and it kept me pushing hard, but I also kept it in its proper place and didn't overly worry or stress about it. I used it as motivation. It's the same today, when I like to surround myself with people who are successful. It motivates me, it helps drive me when I see others striving for success and being successful. It sometimes makes me feel uncomfortable because I want to be where they are. Again, I keep it in its right place and use it for motivation to do what I must do. I don't overly focus on other people or get down on myself. I use competition to fuel me in sustaining the motivation I need over years to continue doing what I do.

Chapter Four:
The Power Of Thinking Without Thinking

"Intuition is the key to everything, in painting, filmmaking, business - everything. I think you could have an intellectual ability, but if you can sharpen your intuition, which they say is emotion and intellect joining together, then a knowingness occurs."
~ David Lynch

What Is Intuition?

Before I get into the connection between intuition and mental toughness, let's first define intuition. Intuition is considered a rapid-fire, unconscious associating process. I combine intuition, gut, and instinct; while they all technically have different definitions, they are interchanged all the time.

Bottom line—this section will look at anything that is not your conscious mind making a decision. When you think about sports and making decisions in the heat of competition, many people will understand exactly what intuition or instincts are; there is a rapid fire of unconscious associative processes that allow people to make quick decisions before their conscious brains have the time to process what is occurring. Most sports rely on this, as

Fortitude

there is no time for the conscious brain to be a part of the equation; it processes things too slowly.

An athlete's ability to perform comes down to their ability to trust their gut, make decisions quickly, and forego conscious thought. When an athlete doesn't trust their gut, they start to overthink things and fail to react quickly enough. One of the reasons our intuition is so powerful is that it processes approximately 20 million pieces of information each second, whereas our conscious mind processes approximately 50 pieces of information. Yet we often forego our intuition and consider our conscious thought process more important.

Really think about that for a minute. Your unconscious processes millions of pieces of information every second, whereas your conscious brain processes a mere 50. That is a huge difference. It's why we get a feeling about something long before we have any evidence to support the feeling we have. Have you ever gone into a situation that just didn't feel right? We don't always know why we feel the way we do because our conscious minds haven't caught up to our intuition. The problem is, often we talk ourselves out of a decision because we need evidence to support it, but we can't possibly collect all the information we want before a decision must be made.

For a long time, intuition and gut decisions weren't really understood, but now scientists are discovering there is a "second brain" in our stomachs. There are so many neurons in the stomach that it's now considered more than just an organ that digests food. It doesn't help with conscious decision-making but it enables us to "feel". It works in conjunction with our conscious brains to allow us to make our way through life.

Sometimes we need our conscious brains to make decisions, to have deeper thought processes when studying math, poetry, philosophy, or mapping out a plan. However, once it's time for action, to be in the present moment, it's time to allow the second brain to take charge and park the conscious mind. Sometimes we also must make a quick decision in the moment and then process it later. In this instance, it is important for both brains to work in conjunction with each other; if done with the appropriate timing, we will be able to use both brains when necessary.

What Does Intuition Have To Do With Mental Toughness?

A big part of mental toughness is being in the flow and not forcing or trying to control things over which you have no control. Intuition is related to mental toughness because when you look at people who have been truly successful, you see that they listen to that small voice within them rather than to their egos or other people, which our egos love to feed off.

When you are striving for something, people will tell you that you can't do it or you will receive messages that you could read as saying this path isn't for you. The intuitive part of you, though, is the part to listen to, the one to say, "This is the path for you," or "It's time to find another path." When you listen to the voice inside of you, you become that much tougher; you develop a much better ability to move through obstacles, barriers, or anything else in your way.

When you tap into your intuition, you tap into a deep knowing and belief. It is important to listen to this side of yourself so you can remain steadfast, focused, and mentally tough. When you listen to some of the most successful people, they often tell stories about how they got cut from a high school team or had a coach, parent, or teacher tell them they wouldn't be able to make it. These successful individuals didn't listen to the noise, they listened to what was being said inside.

Even those who have made it and now make high-pressure decisions don't let the noise distract them. They focus on what they are feeling and the quiet nudge they get. These people know the power of intuition and realize it's a strength. They know not to question it. Whether you are on the journey or have reached the destination, learning to quiet the noise is so important and necessary to becoming and staying mentally tough.

How Can I Develop My Gut And Intuition?

As with anything, it is important to practice! Trusting your gut/intuition is all about using it and seeing how it can benefit you. At first, one of the hardest things is differentiating between your gut and your conscious mind. This is because our intuition is quiet and comes through as a thought, much like our conscious process. It usually comes first and we think it, but before we know it, our conscious brain has chimed in and convinced us that we are wrong.

To get better at using our intuition requires a lot of awareness—being aware of having a thought, of changing it, and of what ends up happening. How many times have you had an instinct to do something, say something, or react to something and then thought your way out of it? We learn by observing our behavior. I tell my clients to pay attention to the small things in everyday life. It's easier to trust your intuition if you use it first for small things that don't matter much or that don't place too much pressure on yourself. With time, it will be easier to learn to trust your intuition with the big things and in situations in which you need rapid processing.

You can also play games that require not knowing something and trying to rely on your gut to help build this skill. For example, a game like Battleship requires someone to give up relying on their conscious brain because it doesn't really help them in the early parts of the game, when there's no information to process on a conscious level.

One time I was participating in a board game night for my brother's birthday. I was paired with one of my sister's friends, and we seemed to be on the same brain wave. When we played Cranium, we seemed to guess everything correctly right away. Could we read each other's minds? Probably not. Instead, I think we had both tapped into our intuition and let it take charge rather than overthinking things. Cranium has parts to it that are timed and that require you to guess what someone is drawing or acting out; it requires rapid processing. Playing games like Battleship or Cranium is a great way to practice intuition; there isn't much on the line, it's fun, and it can help you differentiate between intuition and conscious decision-making.

Other important parts of intuition are trust and being present. Our conscious brains want facts and evidence to support our decisions; this is often why it's so difficult to make decisions that are in the future and that are bigger in nature, like choosing a team to play on or a college to attend. It's impossible to know everything, and because we don't have all "the facts," we can get stuck and not make a decision. We can become very stressed about the situation.

One of the reasons why people always say to visit the campuses of schools before you decide where you want to spend four or more years of your life is because it allows you to tap into your intuition. You get a sense of how you will feel being at that school rather than it being all about what you've read on paper. The more you can put yourself into situations you can feel your way through after you have made all the logical decisions or all the checklists, the easier it will be to trust that feeling even more.

Chapter Five:
The Power Of Focus
(Deep Practice)

"When you are riding, only the race in which you're riding is important."
~ Bill Shoemaker

All You Have Is This Moment

As the title of this chapter suggests, all we have is the moment at hand. Those who can harness the ability to focus on the present moment are the ones who excel. This is true for several reasons. First, to perform to potential, we must be able to focus on the right thing at the right moment. If we don't, we will make mistakes. Being present also means we feel less stress, anxiety, doubt, fear, or anger. In the present moment, there is stillness and peace. Everything we need is at our disposal, and if we can trust ourselves, we'll find a way to do what is necessary in the moment.

Being present is important, but it's becoming increasingly important to not just focus on the present moment but to be able to go deep with our focus. In the past, this was commonplace, something many people experienced and could do. However, the world has changed, and technology is behind this change. Technology is great and helps with many things; however, it is also starting to affect our ability to focus.

Cell phones in particular are causing a shift in the wiring of the brain and how it is able to focus; this is particularly evident with the generation that has grown up with cellphones. The web, social media, constant notifications, and the addiction people have to their phones are changing this skill from something that was common to a rarity and, in so doing, making it even more valuable.

Why is it becoming valuable? Well, the world is changing fast, and those who can learn a new skill quickly and efficiently are the ones who will succeed. This is true in sports and business. To do this, one must reach a place called deep practice/work with one's focus—and this is becoming increasingly harder for individuals to do. First let's define deep practice/work and then talk about what's happening. The definition below comes from a combination of Daniel Coyle's and Cal Newport's work in the area.

Deep practice/work *is a state of distraction-free concentration in which you are working at the edges of your abilities and pushing your cognitive capabilities, putting yourself into a position to make mistakes and, if attended to properly, that will allow you to become smarter and learn faster.*

Fortitude

This means when we get to this place, we can learn skills at an extremely fast rate. Daniel Coyle, author of *The Talent Code*, points out that a young girl, using deep practice, learned a piece of music for piano in an hour—something that would usually take a month to learn. Biologically we must make mistakes and attend to them to grow; if done in a structured and specific way, this can boost the rate at which we learn and grow. However, smartphones are fragmenting our attention into slivers, and if enough time is spent in this fragmented shallow focus, it can become permanent.

Technology has allowed us to spend time on things that don't really matter and that are therefore distracting us from work that requires unbroken concentration. It is degrading our capacity to remain focused. Some people might think that, when they must focus, they can just turn off the cell phone and other distractions; however, our brains are being rewired so that even when we want a deep level of focus, we can't achieve it. We must prepare for the moments when we need to focus.

There is a saying: the master of one or the jack of all trades. The masters of one have focused in depth on one thing, which has allowed them to become masters at it. Depth is required for us to produce our absolute best. The best minds in the world understand this and structure their time so they can achieve it. It's not only about deliberately creating time for depth but also about structuring their lives so their brains can go there when they want. Some of them don't have cell phones or social media accounts and check their emails only at specific times.

Now, I'm not saying you must do this, but if you want to be great at something, you need a certain approach that will allow your brain to focus in a way that allows you to get the most out of your mind and body. For athletes, deliberate practice is key. Deliberate practice, according to Cal Newport, is about being able to put your attention and focus on the specific skills you are trying to improve and receive feedback so you can correct your approach to keep your attention exactly where it is productive.

To help you understand how this works, let's have a little science lesson. When we think a thought or do something physical, a neuron fires. Each time we fire the neuron, myelin grows around it to help it fire faster and more efficiently. Focusing on specific skills forces specific relevant circuits to fire again and again in isolation. The more it fires, the thicker the myelin gets and the stronger and more easily the neuron can fire.

So, whether you are trying to learn a new way of thinking or a new physical skill, the more you can isolate and strengthen the firing of the neuron, the faster you will learn to do what you are trying to do. Producing at a high level is not just about the amount of time spent, but about the time spent plus the intensity of focus. If intensity is there, less time is required. If intensity is not there, more time is required.

Going back to cell phones—the more time someone spends shifting their attention from what they are working on to their cell phone, the stronger the signal becomes and the easier it is for it to fire. This aligns with the fact that many kids have a hard time not being on their cell phones or checking social media every minute. Even when the phone is off, the brain is still wired for distraction and can't get to the depth it needs because it has been trained for shallow work and distraction.

Myths About Focus

To understand focus, it is important to understand the myths associated with it. Below I am going to outline five myths or misnomers that exist when it comes to focus.

Myth #1: Rest = less productivity. Our minds need rest beyond sleep. They need time to recharge so they can focus more intensely when needed. This will increase productivity. In my first book, I mentioned the analogy of our minds with a sprinter. Sprinters use a high amount of energy for a short period of time and then rest. The more intense our focus, the more our minds will need to rest to continue focusing with intensity. If our focus is superficial, it won't need as much time to rest, but we will be less efficient in that mode and there is a higher chance of getting distracted.

It is also through rest and silence that we can discover the best direction to take, which will save time down the road. In a world that has become so stimulating, those who can focus effectively will be the ones who succeed, and allowing one's mind to rest is a key part of this. Allow yourself to become bored; you will be amazed at how productive you become. You will start to focus on what is important instead of on superficial things.

Myth #2: We lose focus. While our focus may not be where it must be, we technically never lose focus. We simply might not be focusing appropriately on what we should be. Performing in sports, business, fitness, or life is about focusing on the right thing at the right time. If you are at practice and are daydreaming, you are still focusing, but your focus should probably be on the coach talking or the drill you are supposed to be doing. If you are in your room and your purpose is to do some creative thinking, daydreaming might be an appropriate type of focus in that moment.

Myth #3: Quantity is better than quality. I think most people know that quality is better than quantity but have a difficult time practicing it. As mentioned earlier it has been shown through research that you can learn something in an hour that usually takes people a month. This also goes for productivity. Time is important for development but more important is how you spend that time. We have this idea that spending more time on something means we worked harder and/or were more productive. It is difficult for people to wrap their brains around the idea of working smarter, not harder. To be more efficient, we must develop the ability for deep practice/work.

Myth #4: You need structure for high levels of focus, creativity, and productivity. I spent most of my free time as a kid on my backyard rink with my siblings. In this environment, I had the ability to be creative and focus on my skill away from structure. I was at my most productive when it was just me out there, goofing around and having fun, getting to try new things, make mistakes, learn from the mistakes, and see if they would be something to use in a game. I believe that children today have lost the art of play in their sport.

What I mean by this is unstructured time that is not "practice" but, instead, time to just have fun, to play or try new skills not for something specific but simply for the fun of the sport—seeing how far you can push your boundaries. Now it seems everything is structured, about creating structure to focus and learn new things. I played pick-up hockey all the time in my backyard rink or on the street. The unfortunate thing is that children often don't have time for this anymore.

Myth #5: You can't be too focused. While focus is important and something many people need to work on due to distractions, there is such a thing as being overly focused. Those who seem to have an innate ability to focus are the ones who tend to run into this problem at times. I am one of those people. I have always had a great ability to focus but it can lead to blinders and sometimes that does not help me. I'm a lot better at this now and at being aware of when this is occurring. When I am overly focused, I can lose track of what is around me, miss information that would be beneficial to see, and lose the ability to tap into and listen to my intuition. We must find a balance between heightened focus and awareness. Each situation will dictate a different combination but they must exist together.

Meditation

In my last book, I presented and discussed various activities that can be done to help with focus control. In this book, I wanted to look in depth into one area I didn't mention in my last book but that is also great for improving focus: meditation. Meditation is something most people reading this book have heard about and potentially tried at some point. Meditation is a big topic to cover and many books would probably be needed to look at it all. What I will cover here looks at how I start introducing this topic to my clients and the goals I set for them through the use of meditation.

There are many benefits to meditation and it has been shown scientifically that it impacts our bodies and minds. Gray matter has been shown to increase in the frontal, auditory, and sensory cortex—areas responsible for focus, shutting down cognition to being aware and present, as well as executive decision-making and working memory. The amygdala, which is associated with fear, anxiety, and stress, has been reduced in size through meditation, lowering the feelings of these emotions. In essence, meditation has been scientifically shown to change our brains so that we get better at focusing, being present, making decisions, and improving memory while simultaneously helping reduce fear, stress, and anxiety.

When I am working with a client, I use meditation for a few reasons. First, I think that given our distracting world, taking time to sit in silence is very beneficial and necessary. Many clients tell me how relaxed it makes them and how much they enjoy this time to sit and reflect.

For many clients, sitting still is very difficult, and if it's difficult to sit for five minutes (the starting time on which I have my clients work), it will be very hard for them to focus on one thing for an extended period of time. Another reason I have clients meditate is for focus control. When we sit in silence, our minds can run wild, which provides an opportunity for someone to learn not to let their mind wander and to bring it back to a focal point. The focal point I use is the breath; it is easy and always there. If someone can learn to focus on their breath and, when their minds try to take them away, gently bring their minds back to their breath, they will be much more able to bring themselves back to the focal point of anything they are doing.

When we think a thought, we usually attach an emotion to it or create a story around it. It is this process that takes a simple thought and makes it distracting or that takes us to the negative mind, which hurts our confidence. A thought is just a thought; everyone has them, even the best athletes and performers. The difference is that those who excel have learned not to build a story or emotions around the thought and to simply bring themselves back to what is right in front of them and important in that moment. Mediation helps with this. Meditation is also great for acquiring an overall calm mind.

Fortitude

The more consistently we meditate over a period of time, the more it will impact and help us even while we are away from meditation.

Many people try to be calm and bring their focus back under high-pressure situations with little luck. It usually makes things worse as they start to get frustrated. To have the focus you want requires consistent work, and meditation is one of the many things you can do. If you wish to find other ways to help with focus, take a look at my first book, *Get Into the Zone*, which has some great tips and tools for gaining better control of your focus.

Chapter Six:
The Ability To Refocus

"We can't predict the future, we can only get ready for the unpredictable."
~ John McHahon

Flexibility Is Not Just For Your Body

While all mental skills have their challenges, refocusing is one that stands out. I would say that the ability to refocus is the second most difficult skill for mental toughness—second only to confidence. Confidence greatly affects our ability to refocus, and the ability to refocus greatly affects the other skills mentioned in this book. If you can't refocus once your focus has strayed, it doesn't matter how much motivation you have or how good you are at making decisions. You can have all the motivation in the world but if it's not directed at the right thing, it doesn't matter.

This chapter is called "Flexibility is not just for your body" because that is exactly what one's ability to refocus is all about. The mind must be flexible enough to move from one thing to another. If it isn't flexible, it becomes that much harder to focus on what is important.

Fortitude

An example I use to help my clients understand shifting from one type of focus to another is that of a manual car. Now, hopefully I'm not completely dating myself, as I know manual cars are not as popular as they once were. If you've ever driven a manual car, you know the difference between how two cars shift gears. If you were to try to shift gears in a car made in the '80s as compared to one made today, you'd encounter a difference. Today's car would shift smoothly, effortlessly, and easily. The car from the '80s would most likely stick, and you would need to put in some effort to get it from one gear to the next. Our minds must be like the manual car of today: able to shift our focus appropriately and refocus on what is important.

What stops the mind from being flexible? I see two main causes. One is anger and the other is performance anxiety. Anger forces people to focus outwardly and on the source of their anger. What can then happen is that the person becomes fixated on the anger and no longer on what is important. They lose the ability to shift to what they need to focus on because they are focused instead on the source of their anger. Performance anxiety, for its part, causes a person to focus inwardly on worry, doubt, and fear. This too affects a person's ability to refocus because the performance anxiety has pulled them inward and they can't make the necessary adjustments to what they should focus on in that moment.

Thus, people with higher levels of anger and performance anxiety tend to have more difficulty refocusing. When things don't go their way, people with higher levels of anger and performance anxiety are greatly affected by these emotions and loose the ability to bring themselves back. This is hard because when they need the ability to refocus the most, doing so is most difficult. For these people, getting better at refocusing is about dealing with the emotions of anger and performance anxiety; with time, they can have a better handle on learning to bring back their focus.

The Challenges Of Refocusing

Beyond what I mentioned previously, the challenges of refocusing are confidence, control, and the ability to let go of mistakes, resentment, and imperfections. These all affect one's ability to refocus. When people are more confident, they tend to feel that they have more control over things. This can be beneficial and necessary for refocusing because when something happens, such as a setback or mistake that pulls away our focus, we must feel that we have some form of control over our lives and that we can bring ourselves back to feel that, no matter what happens, we will learn from it and fight.

Fortitude

It's the feeling that we can take charge of our lives. Confidence also helps individuals view situations or feelings as temporary and able to be overcome. When we view things as temporary, it is much easier to let go and refocus where we need to.

However, when confidence is low, there is a lower sense of control, a feeling that things happen to an individual and that what happens is permanent. When someone feels like things happen to them and they are not temporary, they can get caught up in the setbacks or mistakes and have difficulty bringing themselves back to what matters and what is in their control. The interesting thing is that those who feel they have control and who view things that happen as temporary benefit from refocusing; however, I have found that this can also cause them to have difficulty refocusing because the need for control gets placed on things that can't be controlled.

One of the most important abilities someone must develop to refocus is giving up control at times and to trust the process. The giving up of control actually gives them more control. This is extremely hard to do for many individuals who like control. They will find ways to gain control, and if they don't see any way to do so, they will look to things that aren't controllable or will become frustrated and angry.

There must be a healthy balance between feeling in control of one's life, seeing things as temporary, both good and bad, and simultaneously being able to let go, trust, and have faith in what one cannot see. The quote at the beginning of this chapter by John McHahon says is all "We can't predict the future, we can only get ready for the unpredictable." This is key to your ability to stay flexible and refocus.

You must prepare as much as you can, but once you have prepared, you must be able to let go and trust that you are ready for whatever comes your way and stay present in the moment. That is what will allow you to continually stay focused on what is important and bring yourself back when you lose focus.

What Can I Do To Help Myself Refocus Better?

There are several things that can help you refocus. What you choose will depend on the factor causing you to experience problems refocusing. First, if confidence is holding you back, you must start there. Build your confidence to a point where it becomes easier to feel in control, trust yourself, and view things as temporary.

This will take time. Confidence is not a quick fix; it can take years, but if you are ready to put in the work, it will be well worth it. You need confidence to refocus; without it, you will always struggle with this skill. Confidence will also help if you are dealing with anxiety. While there are other things that can cause anxiety, low confidence is one of them. The more confidence you have, the less anxiety you will feel. With less anxiety, you will spend less time focused on worry, fear, and doubt and be able to bounce back.

If you think anger is the source of your difficulty with refocusing, you must spend some time figuring out what is making you angry. Often, high levels of confidence can create anger because they usually accompany a high sense of control, and when you are trying to control things and they are not going your way, anger is the common emotional response.

For most people who don't fall into the above categories, the way to get better at refocusing is to get better at letting go of mistakes, resentment, and perfection. The world that exists is full of messages telling us about being perfect and to not make mistakes. We must make mistakes; we can't be perfect. Once you can come to accept this, it becomes easier to move on. This is what allows us to refocus.

We spend so much time and energy as human beings on things that have happened or that we think might happen in the future that we lose what is happening right now. A big reason for this is the emotional attachment we have created to the past and future; we've created it less to the present. Emotions are strong, and they will pull our focus; the more emotional we become, the more focused we are on something and the harder it is for us to shift and find a better use for our focus in that moment. Learn to accept, trust, and let go so that you have the ability to see what is appropriate to focus on in a given moment.

A final strategy that can help with refocusing is creating routines or a structure around the need to shift your focus. This is a great thing to do if you know you're shifting your focus from one thing to the next and you know it will be happening. This can be done with things large or small. For example, I was talking to a client about a friend of his who is in the military. When he comes back from deployment, he spends approximately two weeks in an apartment, then rejoins his wife and kids. Many people might wonder why he does this. He has already been gone for a long period of time, but this allows him to shift gears from being deployed to being back in normal life. It increases the quality of the time he has with his family.

I had another client who was getting ready to go to an NFL training camp. He usually left just beforehand to maximize his time with his family. While working with me, he started thinking about taking an extra couple of days to make the journey (he was driving) to help him shift his mindset from

Fortitude

being at home with his family in the off season to getting back into full football mode. This gave him the necessary time to head into camp and preseason with the focus he needed at that time.

These may seem like two significant examples, but shifting gears and refocusing on something else also happen every day. Going from school to practice and then from practice to homework, or from work to family life, we must find ways to make the transitions. That can be through routines, finding ways to close out what you are doing before moving on to the next thing. For example, if you are doing work, create a shutting-down process that allows you to close things out or make notes about what you will need to pick up later.

That way, you can walk away with less mental residue than if you simply rush out the door and head to the next thing. We need ways to have less mental residue, which is having things present from what we were doing before moving into the next thing we are doing. A big part of what keeps us from being present is still thinking about what we were doing before or thinking about what we must do next. Finding ways to minimize this extra thinking will help.

Chapter Seven: Mindfulness

"Feelings come and go like clouds in a windy sky. Conscious breathing is my anchor."
~ Thich Nhat Hanh

What Is Mindfulness?

I like to define mindfulness as the ability to be aware and present at the same time. We must have the ability to be aware of ourselves—what we are feeling, where we are in time and space—and at the same time be present in the moment. Being mindful is not easy; we like to be distracted, to ignore feelings, or over identify with them and make things bigger or smaller than they really are. To truly be mindful, we must know ourselves, our minds, and how they work. This is the awareness component of mindfulness.

I have worked with many people over the years and wanting to be more aware of their inner dimension is one of the reasons they come to see me. It is also one of my goals. We are all different and we ultimately are the experts when it comes to ourselves—no one else. I may know a lot, know how to help someone perform at a higher level, and interpret performance assessments to help me know someone, but really, at the end of the day, whomever I'm working with is the expert on themselves.

I am merely a guide to help them discover themselves and think about things in new ways to open their thought process and discover what they must know to get the most out of themselves. Those I have worked with who are more mindful and thoughtful about themselves are the ones who succeed and develop faster. When someone is interested in their own self-development, beyond the work I am doing with them, it only helps our work and progress.

Many people don't want to invest in themselves because they are worried about what they will find out or feel if they go down that path. It's not easy because with the good experiences also come the not-so-comfortable realizations. To succeed we often must go through difficult moments, through self-reflection, and that isn't for everyone. However, it is for those who really want to succeed and who aren't afraid to see and confront their shortcomings. To know oneself is the key to success; it allows us to be more mindful.

Why Do I Need To Figure Out My Own Mind?

Being mindful is the key to success because when we understand ourselves and how we tick, we can make great change. Without it we simply have a bunch of information and tools at our disposal with no way of using them. Some people go blindly through life not understanding themselves, always being the same—for example, the victim, the bully, the egoist. People who continue acting in the same way will always get the same result.

Often these are people who aren't even aware that they can choose to do things differently. They may complain about their lot in life. They may think they're more capable than they are. Some may undervalue their abilities. It doesn't matter how good you are at something, if you have a low level of awareness about who you are and what you bring to the situation, the more you will struggle to succeed and get what you want.

I have a client who knows that others experience him as aggressive and not open. Before he started going down the path of understanding himself, he thought everyone else had the problem, not him. He didn't understand what he was doing that made people a little put off by him. This affected him in a number of ways because the people in his world who had an authority position didn't like how they experienced him. It cost him a lot.

Now he is in a position where being open is a must for what he does. Since he has done the work to understand this aspect of himself, he has become aware and mindful. This has given him the ability to present himself as open in situations in which he knows he needs this quality. Without this new awareness and mindfulness, he could have continued behaving in the same way over and over again, constantly getting the same unsatisfactory results in different situations, never positioning himself to get what he wants and where he wants.

There is a great quote from Sri Nisargadatta Maharaj: "You cannot transcend what you do not know. To go beyond yourself, you must know yourself." We bring ourselves into every situation we experience, and no matter what is in front of us we act the same way we always have until we bring some awareness and mindfulness to the situation. It is imperative for people to have some level of self-awareness if they truly want to make changes that will allow them to succeed and to do so in a way with which they will be happy.

How Is Mindfulness Related To Mental Toughness?

One of the most difficult things in the world is to be truly present. As a society, we like to be distracted, as it makes things easier. It can seem easier if we don't look at our own feelings or aren't really present in a moment. We can think that being mindful is only for those who are mentally tough. To take the step of seeing things you maybe didn't want to see or be aware of, to be able to let go of all the chaos and noise around you and just be still and present is difficult.

It is one of the reasons why meditation is so difficult and one of the hardest things to start doing. My experience with clients has shown me that those who do meditate find it difficult at first, but if they stick with it they are the ones who rank higher on the mental toughness scale. Many clients stop progressing because working on their goals is not easy; they find many excuses for why they stopped, but the real reason is often that they had difficulty with being mindful and present. This says a lot about how mindful they are as they go throughout their day.

So, I strongly suggest—if this is something you struggle with or if you want to know whether being mindful is something you might struggle with—that you start meditating and see how well you do at keeping up with it. If you have difficulty, meditation is definitely something to start implementing into your life to help build your mental toughness. If meditation is something that comes easily to you, this part of mental toughness might not be something you have to work on. I would still recommend meditating for all its other benefits, but you could put more time and energy into other components of mental toughness.

There is a program on Showtime called *Billions*. One of the stars of the show is Daniel Lewis,

Fortitude

who plays a billionaire who owns Axe Capital, a hedge fund. There is a moment in the first season when someone is describing him and says he has "monk-like discipline," that not everyone could have all the information and moving parts swirling around in their brain and remain as calm and steadfast as he does.

Well, in the show they have him meditating as well as having a performance coach on staff to help him and his employees continuously perform at their highest level. Being able to have many moving parts and information all at once and to remain calm, focused, and present requires a strong mentality, so if you are ready to go to that next level, make sure you are ready to be more mindful and present.

Conclusion

"Pressure is a privilege. If you don't have any pressure, it means you have no chance."
~ Mike Babcock

How To Apply The Building Blocks Of Mental Toughness To Your Life

As you can see from this book, mental toughness is not just one thing but is made up of many components. You might be good at one area but need to bolster others. So, it's important that you take some time to really evaluate which components you are good at and must focus on maintaining and which components you must build and develop so you can gain more mental toughness.

Mental toughness is not just for high-pressure situations; while it's important in such situations, day-to-day living also requires it and gives us many moments to build and practice our mental toughness. If we use our daily lives to do this building and practicing, it becomes easier to have mental toughness when we need it in critical moments. Mental toughness is like a muscle in the body; the more you work it and strengthen it, the more developed it will be and the easier it will be to tap into.

As I mentioned at the beginning, these might not be all the parts of mental toughness; they are just the ones I have experienced as the most dominant and the things I seem to spend the most time working on with clients. If there is another area on which you need to work and that you think will help with your mental toughness, do so. Let this be a starting point; take what you need from this book and expand upon it in such a way that the information works best for you.

Also know that it is important to keep monitoring and working on your mental toughness; life changes all the time and you never know when you will need that next level. Stay adaptable and know that sometimes there might be lulls when you don't need to work on it as much. However, I have found that the moment someone thinks they no longer need to work on a skill, they actually need to do so the most, as they will most likely need that skill soon.

I hope you have enjoyed this book and found it valuable and useful as you continue moving towards your goals, your dreams, and the success you want. My intention was to take the many ideas, approaches, and things I have seen along the way and put them in one place in a concise and to-the-point manner. I hope that if you found one area of the book intriguing or want to learn more about it, you will do some research and dig deeper. This is by no means the be-all and end-all for mental toughness but I think it is a good start. I thank you for taking the time to read the book. If you have any questions, my contact information is at the back of the book. I wish you all the best on your journey.

Notes

Chapter 1
1. Definition of Mental Toughness - See Jones, Hanton & Connaughton (2002) *What is this thing called Mental Toughness? An Investigation of elite sport performers.*
2. Dr. Robert Bell *The Hinge: The Importance of Mental Toughness*

Chapter 2
1. Definition of confidence - See *Dictionary.com*
2. Dr. Robert Bell *The Hinge: The Importance of Mental Toughness*
3. Amy Cuddy - See TedTalk 2012 *Your Body Language May Shape Who You Are*
4. Amy Cuddy *Presence: Bringing your Boldest Self to you Biggest Challenges*
5. Daniel Coyle *Talent Code: Greatness Isn't Born It"s Grown*
6. Self fulfilling prophecy see Kassin, Fein & Markus (2011) *Social Psychology 8th Edition*
7. Brené Brown - *Gifts of Imperfection: Let Go of Who You Think You're Supposed to Be and Embrace Who You Are*
8. Information on trust and humility can be found more in depth in Stephen M.R. Covey's book *The Speed of Trust: The One Thing That Changes Everything*

9. Brené Brown *Boundaries* a video that can be found on YouTube

Chapter 3
1. Definition of motivation see Daniel Coyle's *The Talent Code: Greatness Isn't Born It's Grown.*
2. For a comprehensive and scholarly look at motivation, see Carol Dweck and Andrew Eliot, eds., *The Handbook of Competence and Motivation* (New York: Guilford Press, 2005).
3. For Carol Dweck's study measuring the power of one line of praise, see A. Cimpian et al., "Subtle Linguistic Clues Affect Children's Motivation," *Psychological Science* 18 (2007), 314-16.
4. Dweck is also the author of *Mindset: The New Psychology of Success* (New York: Random House, 2006).

Chapter 4
1. Definition of Intuition see *Learning Theories: An Educational Perspective* 6th Edition by Dale H Schunk
2. For more on thinking without thinking see Malcholm Gladwell's *Blink: Power of Thinking Without Thinking*
3. Subconscious versus conscious information see *Cognitive Psychology* 6th Edition by Robert J. Sternberg and Karin Sternberg

Fortitude

Chapter 5
1. Information on deep work/practice see *Deep Work: Rules For Focused Success in a Distracted World* by Cal Newport and *The Talent Code: Greatness Isn't Born It's Grown* by Daniel Coyle

Chapter 6
1. For more information on mental residue and shutting down routine see *Deep Work: Rules For Focused Success in a Distracted World* by Cal Newport

Chapter 7
1. For more on self development see *Ignite The Third Factor: How Do You Get People Committed to Reaching Their Full Potential?* by Dr. Peter Jensen

Contact Information

I am always happy to help in anyway I can, so if you are in need of more advice or help being pointed in the right direction please feel free to give me a call or send me an email and I will be happy to speak with you free of charge! Thank you so much for reading this book.

Kate Allgood
www.qpathlete.com
5752 Oberlin Dr Ste 223
San Diego, CA 92121
Phone:619-446-6846
Email: kate@qpathlete.com

www.ingramcontent.com/pod-product-compliance
Lightning Source LLC
Chambersburg PA
CBHW071728040426
42446CB00011B/2264